THE MASSIVE DIPLODOCUS

BY PETER FINN

DINOSAUR WORLD

Enslow
PUBLISHING

DISCOVER!

Please visit our website, www.enslow.com. For a free color catalog of all our high-quality books, call toll free 1-800-398-2504 or fax 1-877-980-4454.

Library of Congress Cataloging-in-Publication Data

Names: Finn, Peter, 1978- author.
Title: The massive diplodocus / Peter Finn.
Description: New York : Enslow Publishing, [2022] | Series: Dinosaur world
  | Includes index.
Identifiers: LCCN 2020049031 (print) | LCCN 2020049032 (ebook) | ISBN
  9781978521162 (library binding) | ISBN 9781978521148 (paperback) | ISBN
  9781978521155 (set) | ISBN 9781978521179 (ebook)
Subjects: LCSH: Diplodocus–Juvenile literature.
Classification: LCC QE862.S3 F5576 2022 (print) | LCC QE862.S3 (ebook) |
  DDC 567.913–dc23
LC record available at https://lccn.loc.gov/2020049031
LC ebook record available at https://lccn.loc.gov/2020049032

Published in 2022 by
Enslow Publishing
101 West 23rd Street, Suite #240
New York, NY 10011

Copyright © 2022 Enslow Publishing

Designer: Sarah Liddell
Interior Layout: Rachel Rising
Editor: Therese Shea

Illustrations by Jeffrey Mangiat
Science Consultant: Darla Zelenitsky, Ph.D.,
Assistant Professor of Dinosaur Paleontology at the University of Calgary, Canada

Photo credits: Cover, pp. 1, 5, 7, 9, 11, 13, 15, 17, 19, 21 (rock border) SirinR/Shutterstock.com; pp. 2, 4, 6, 8, 10, 12, 14, 16, 18, 20, 22, 23, 24 (background) altanaka/Shutterstock.com; pp. 5, 11, 13, 17, 19 (egg) fotoslaz/Shutterstock.com.

Portions of this work were originally authored by Thomas George and published as Diplodocus. All new material this edition authored by Peter Finn.

Printed in the United States of America

Some of the images in this book illustrate individuals who are models. The depictions do not imply actual situations or events.

CPSIA compliance information: Batch #CSENS22. For further information contact Enslow Publishing, New York, New York, at 1-800-398-2504.

Find us on

CONTENTS

Boldface words appear in Words to Know.

HELLO, DIPLODOCUS!

Diplodocus was a large dinosaur. It was about as long as two buses! It belonged to a dinosaur group called sauropods (SOHR-eh-podz). All were big and walked on four legs. They had a long neck and tail. Sauropods were plant eaters.

HOW TO SAY
DIPLODOCUS:
DIH-PLAH-DEH-KUHS

5

WHEN AND WHERE?

Diplodocus lived more than 145 **million** years ago. Scientists have learned a lot about it by studying its **fossils**. *Diplodocus* fossils have been found in western North America. Scientists discovered these fossils in Montana, Wyoming, Utah, and Colorado.

BIG BODY

Diplodocus was one of the longest land animals ever! The biggest species, or kind, was over 100 feet (30 m) long. It had a long neck and an even longer tail. Its tail was made up of 80 bones in all.

LONG NECK →

LONG TAIL →

9

FIGHTING BACK

Diplodocus moved slowly because it was so large. Faster dinosaurs may have hunted them. However, scientists think *Diplodocus*'s tail was a **defense**. Some believe it could **whip** its tail at a speed of 800 miles (1,287 km) per hour!

ONE OF DIPLODOCUS'S PREDATORS WAS ALLOSAURUS, SHOWN HERE.

11

PLANT EATER

Such a big animal needed a lot of food. *Diplodocus* ate hundreds of pounds of plants each day! Scientists have studied their teeth. They think *Diplodocus* ate softer plants and leaves. It didn't have a powerful bite, like other dinosaurs did.

ANOTHER NAME
FOR PLANT EATER
IS HERBIVORE
(HER-BIH-VOHR).

13

SPECIAL TEETH

Diplodocus had about 40 small teeth in the front of its mouth. The teeth pointed forward a bit. This might mean *Diplodocus* **scraped** leaves off branches. It had no back teeth to break up its food. It **digested** food in its body slowly.

14

ABOUT 40
LITTLE TEETH

REACHING HIGHER

Diplodocus might have lifted its long neck to reach leaves up high. But it couldn't hold its neck up long. Some scientists think its tail helped it **balance** on its back legs. That way, it could reach even higher!

DIPLODOCUS
MOSTLY ATE PLANTS
NEAR THE GROUND.

17

EGGS

Diplodocus mothers laid eggs about the size of a grapefruit. The eggs may have been laid in a pit covered by plants. *Diplodocus* babies **hatched** between 2 and 3 months later. *Diplodocus* laid few eggs at a time to keep them safe from predators.

DIPLODOCUS EGGS WERE SMALL FOR AN ANIMAL THAT BIG.

HERDS

Some scientists think *Diplodocus* lived in herds. This would have kept them safer from predators. Herds could guard young *Diplodocus* too. Imagine a big group of these large dinosaurs. There's much more to learn about the huge *Diplodocus*!

DIPLODOCUS

LARGE SAUROPOD

ABOUT 40
TEETH

LONG TAIL

PLANT EATER

MOVED SLOWLY

WALKED ON
FOUR LEGS

WORDS TO KNOW

balance Being able to stay in place without falling.

defense A way of guarding against an enemy.

digest To break down food inside the body so that the body can use it.

fossil The hardened marks or remains of plants and animals that formed over thousands or millions of years.

hatch To break open or come out of.

million A thousand thousands, or 1,000,000.

scrape To remove by repeated strokes with something sharp or rough.

whip To move something very quickly and with force.

FOR MORE INFORMATION

BOOKS

Allatson, Amy. *Diplodocus*. New York, NY: Kidhaven Publishing, 2018.

Hansen, Grace. *Diplodocus*. Minneapolis, MN: Abdo Kids, 2018.

Sabelko, Rebecca. *Diplodocus*. Minneapolis, MN: Bellwether Media, 2020.

WEBSITES

Diplodocus
www.nhm.ac.uk/discover/dino-directory/diplodocus.html
See how big this dinosaur was compared to a human.

Diplodocus Facts for Kids
www.sciencekids.co.nz/sciencefacts/dinosaurs/diplodocus.html
Read some quick facts about *Diplodocus*.

INDEX

TITLES IN THIS SERIES

THE **FEROCIOUS** TYRANNOSAURUS REX

THE **FIERCE** VELOCIRAPTOR

THE **HUGE** ALLOSAURUS

THE **MASSIVE** DIPLODOCUS

THE **MIGHTY** STEGOSAURUS

THE **POWERFUL** TRICERATOPS

ISBN: 9781978521148
6-pack ISBN: 9781978521155

Enslow
PUBLISHING

9 781978 521148